Colum Sands

Between the

Earth and the Sky

Illustrated by Colum McEvoy

First published by Cottage Publications,
Donaghadee, N. Ireland 2000.
Copyrights Reserved.
© Text Colum Sands 2000
© Music Elm Grove Music 2000
© Paintings Colum McEvoy 2000
All rights reserved.
No part of this book may be reproduced or
stored on any media without the express
written permission of the publishers.
Design & origination in Northern Ireland.
Printed & bound in Singapore.

ISBN 1 900935 19 8

Foreword

Colum Sands is a gifted performer who is renowned both as a soloist and as a member of the Sands Family – one of Ireland's best loved musical groups. He is also one of the world's finest songwriters. His songs look both inwards and outwards but like most great artists he draws his primary inspiration from his immediate environment – from the rich and colorful tapestry of local life in his native County Down. Colum's songs act as portals into the daily lives of people whose world has been shaped for generations by a complex mosaic of historical forces which created deep and often tragic social divisions. But tensions are generally mediated in daily life by neighbourliness and good humor and Colum's deeply insightful and eternally optimistic voice chronicles his community with compassion and a sly but always gentle wit that is positively Chaucerian in its tone and outlook.

Colum McEvoy's crafted water colors are a perfect complement to the songs – an extraordinary union of sound, text and image that makes this collection wonderful and unique.

Mick Moloney
Professor of Ethnomusicology
University of New York

Contents

Introduction

"Do you think that songs can bring about change?" It's early in the morning. Too early to be out of bed and thinking of answers to questions like that. It's also too early for breakfast, especially if you like the kind of breakfast that's surrounded by peace, calm and only the most understanding of company. Still, as the saying goes, it's bad that can't be worse and, even though we've only had three hours sleep and there's a language barrier with our hosts at the breakfast table, words seem unnecessary and the question can be left to hang in the air for a while, floating along with the aroma of freshly baked bread and the wonderful smell of coffee yet to be tasted. My eyes are still only half-open but I think I'm starting to enjoy this. Yes, there's the sugar, in it goes, and that will be the milk jug, into the cup with the white liquid as well. One final stir with the spoon and the coffee sets out on that perilous voyage betwixt the cup and the lip. And then, in less than a second, the proverb suddenly leaps into life. Without warning the door is flung open and we're blinded by the lights and the bustle of a television crew complete with an interpreter. A furry microphone in my face faithfully captures the sound of coffee spilling over the leg of my trousers as the camera lens nimbly avoids the interpreter's hesitation to translate the words that escape from my still unbreakfasted lips. "Sorry to interrupt you my friends, please forgive us, but it's not often that we have Irish visitors here, most interesting for our viewers to see you eat breakfast, and yes, what's your expression, "A change is as good as a rest, is it right?" "Yes, that's right, that's right, a change is as good as a rest."

One half of my untasted coffee is now well on its way down to my socks and, as I survey the other half, most of it spilt into a surprised saucer, I wonder if that television interviewer would believe just how much change and how little rest I have seen since yesterday. Let me turn the clock back twenty four hours.

c.1968. L to R: Tom, Colum, Anne, Ben, Eugene

Amidst all these changes, music flowed through our house and touched most parts of our lives. My father played the fiddle, my mother played the accordion and they both sang. Neighbours and relations would often drop in to see us in the evenings or on Sundays to exchange songs, tunes and stories. A distant relation called Lizzie O Hagan would arrive now and again on warm summer days, riding an elegant black bicycle. She was a devout and pious woman and if she had any weakness at all for material things, then it was for the piano, which rested quietly in our sitting room.

Before the dust of her bicycle tyres had settled, she would be in that room, the parlour as we called it, and having first performed the ritual of removing her black coat and scarf, she would proceed to undress the piano, removing the lid and the front coverings to reveal the dizzying array of hammers, strings and internal organs. She would next produce a lever and a little wedge, which muted certain strings, and then, with great patience, she would set about fine tuning the instrument. Like many other pianos in the country, it was tuned a semi- tone below concert pitch, there were some people who maintained that if an old piano was tuned up to concert pitch it might explode and maybe take any bystanders with it to eternity. Be that as it may, Lizzie knew how to tune a piano and how to play it as well and, later on in the evening she would be vamping away to reels and jigs played on the fiddle by my father and sometimes my Uncle Hugh as well. Between the tunes there would be songs, everyone was expected to do a turn, and it was at these times that any children in the company would realise the importance of having a song or two at the tip of the tongue. Along with the old songs that we heard from our parents and neighbours, there were the new songs coming out of the radio and the ones that we were beginning to write ourselves. Unaccompanied singing was the norm although sometimes my sister Mary and brother Ben would add their piano playing to a song or tune. Then one day during the 1960s, my brother Hugh brought a guitar home from college and things were never quite the same again. At first, my father and Lizzie O Hagan expressed doubt as to whether it was a real instrument at all but soon that guitar was being played along with songs old and new by my brother Tommy and myself, Ben was also playing fiddle, my younger brother Eugene was playing mandolin and banjo and sister Anne was singing. From sessions at home we moved out to local concerts and eventually to Dublin where we won a national competition with a prize of three weeks in New York. We started off playing in The Old Shieling Clubs over there in the Bronx and Queens and then, a few months later, found ourselves appearing in Carnegie Hall. And from there to many countries around the world including that visit to Berlin and the early morning breakfast that I mentioned earlier.

Many fasts have been broken since that morning under the glare of television lights in Berlin and the candlelit breakfast with the three legged cat in Mayobridge, but music and travelling have remained part of the staple diet in the days which have followed. And that's a good thing, especially in these days when life threatens to become more and more hectic with the passing of each year. As I write these notes to meet a publishers deadline on this morning in May 2000, I hope that some of the songs and pictures which you'll find on the pages ahead will help to bring life back to normal speed or, to put it in another way, help to slow us down in the mad rush through the great art gallery of life.

Some of the songs reach back to childhood memories, many of them remain close to home and yet could never have been written had I not left my own land to travel to other countries. No better way than travel to bring a smile of understanding to your face as you learn to see yourself through the eyes of others. A Japanese woman who I met after a concert in Palo Alto earlier this year explained to me that the song 'Looking the Loan of a Spade' would make perfect sense in Japan. She also added to my ongoing education by informing me that in her eyes, all non-oriental people looked exactly the same and she had great difficulty in noticing any difference at all in their faces. On the other hand, Wolfgang Engelberger, a teacher and cabaret artist in Ravensburg was convinced that the faces he saw in 'Newry Market' were exactly the same as those in his local market and so he translated the song into German. Gerhard Van Maasaakers in Holland heard something in 'Whatever you say, say nothing' and translated it into Dutch.

2000. L to R: Colum. Anne, Tom, Ben

The list goes on but I'll let it stop with a man who came up to me just as I went on stage in Whitby three days ago. He asked me if I'd sing the song, 'The Last House in Our Street'. He told me that he was an ex-British soldier and that this song, of a situation seen through the eyes of a child, had changed him forever. Little meetings like these help me to answer a question that was posed at an early morning breakfast table many years ago. It is later in the day now and I've had time to think. Yes, songs can bring about change. And, as I look forward to the rest of the day, I hope that changes will always bring about songs.

The Man with the Cap

A song from the pace and place of growing up, Ryan Road, near Mayobridge in County Down

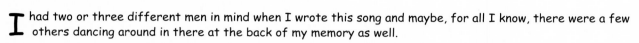

I had two or three different men in mind when I wrote this song and maybe, for all I know, there were a few others dancing around in there at the back of my memory as well.

What I am sure of though is that one of those men was an uncle of mine, a great man who, as far as I can remember, never travelled more than about ten miles from home in his life. He took a big black bicycle with him at all times, I often watched him walking along beside it and came to the conclusion that he took his bicycle with him as much for company as for transport.

It was a fine strong bicycle with the standard black bag behind the seat, (the exact size for carrying a loaf of bread), a three speed gear system, dynamo lighting and a decoy bicycle pump. The decoy pump, which wouldn't have blown up a paper bag, was there merely to confuse and perplex any would-be thieves, the "good" pump travelled safely and snugly in the inside pocket of my uncle's great coat.

Sunday was the day when his bicycle was most likely to leave Burren and come purring along the Ryan Road before turning down the lane to our house. Uncle Patrick never came in through the door without a generous bagful of minutely detailed and hugely entertaining accounts of who and what he had encountered on his travels that day. His powers of observation taught me from an early age that a five-mile journey by bicycle could be more exciting and colourful than a journey of three hundred miles by car or five thousand miles by plane.

At the end of some of those plane journeys, I have found myself singing this song in many different countries and, wherever I go, people often say to me afterwards, "I know a man just like the one you were singing about in that song." So, it would seem that there are many "men with caps" out there, each one with his own story to tell.

This song is for all of them and I hope that someday it may help someone, somewhere to take the time to stop and listen to one of those stories.

The Man with the Cap

Words & Music Colum Sands © Elm Grove Music

They say he was the strangest man you'd e-ver want to meet, He didn't like the towns at all and he

kept to the qui-et streets, But most-ly he was in the fields, he al-ways wore a cap, The

same one for a Sun-day as for briar-din' up a gap, And no one has a pho-to of this

man No one seemed to know his plan – He was lone-ly as a ba-by and as

gen-tle as a child, And it seems he of-ten spoke of Os-car Wilde.

They say he was the strangest man you'd ever want to meet,
He didn't like the towns at all and he kept to the quiet streets,
But mostly he was in the fields, he always a cap,
The same one for a Sunday as for briardin' up a gap,*
And no one has a photo of this man

No one seemed to know his plan
He was lonely as a baby and as gentle as a child
And it seems he often spoke of Oscar Wilde.

I mind we used to see him on the quiet summer nights
Standing by the roadside like a rabbit in the lights
He'd never wave just nod his head, he always a wore a tie
Some people said that he was odd and others said, just shy,
And no one has a photo of this man.

It seems he loved a girl one time but she must have gone away,
Perhaps he was too quiet or too different in his ways
For he never bothered after that, got careless with his looks
Forgot to shave for seven years and took to reading books
And no one has a photo of this man.

I saw him in the cornfield, sowing with his hand,
He understood the weather and he understood the land,
He always wore what once had been a three-piece navy suit,
The same one for the sowing as for standing up the stooks,#
And no one has a photo of this man.

They say he'd stand for hours, gazing at the hills,
His bicycle beside him both of them as still,
As statues in the sunset and no one knew his mind,
But when he died they said that he was kind.

We laid him down this morning; the rain was falling fast,
Those who thought they knew him were with him to the last,
The priest was sprinkling prayers and holy water in the rain
And we said, we'll hardly ever see the likes of him again,
And no one has a photo of this man.

No one seemed to know his plan
He was lonely as a baby and as gentle as a child
And it seems he often spoke of Oscar Wilde.

*briardin' up a gap: filling a gap or hole in a wall or fence
with thorny branches or briars.

#stooks: four sheaves of corn/oats or hay stood together
on their ends and supporting each other.

The March Ditch

A farming community, united and divided.

The earliest horizons I can remember were the hawthorn hedges which stitched together the small fields of the farm where I grew up on the Ryan Road, near Mayobridge in County Down. The hedges were taller than I was but although I couldn't see over them, I could see through them in winter and peer into them in Spring and early summer as I searched for birds nests with my brothers and sisters. Hedges and stone walls also marked the dividing line or "March Ditch" between two properties. They were often a cause of dispute at local level just as a border might be at international level. The neighbours on the far side of our march ditch did the same work in the fields as we did and indeed we often helped each other out at harvest time. But they 'dug with the other foot' as the saying goes and so, although we played and worked in the fields together, we went our separate ways on Sundays and on schooldays. This song is about growing up and trying to figure out why and how we were supposed to be different. Apart from our escape from work in the fields on the 15th of August and their day off on the 12th of July, I thought that we all seemed to be more or less the same. Many years after the events described in this song, I read an interesting quote where someone had said that if you wanted to create maximum mischief in any society, you would take children and separate them into two groups at an early age of say four or five. You would keep them apart as much as possible, particularly in their education and you would make sure to teach them slightly different versions of history. Then, when they reach their late teens, let them get together again and just stand back to see what happens. The kind of thing that can happen is referred to in the fifth verse of The March Ditch but I still think that this is a song of hope.

The March Ditch

Words & Music Colum Sands © Elm Grove Music

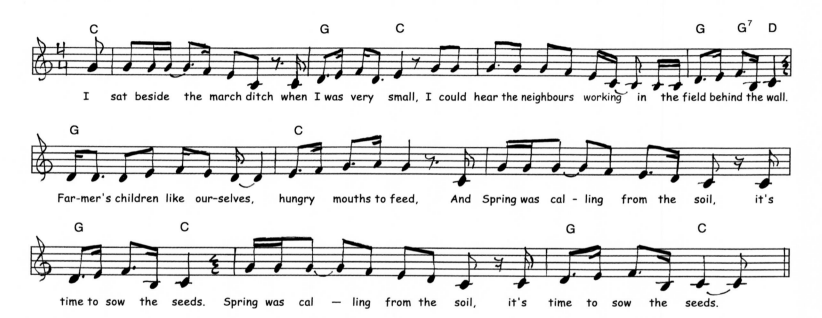

I sat beside the march ditch when I was very small, I could hear the neighbours working in the field behind the wall.

Far-mer's children like our-selves, hungry mouths to feed, And Spring was cal - ling from the soil, it's

time to sow the seeds. Spring was cal — ling from the soil, it's time to sow the seeds.

I sat beside the march ditch when I was very small,
I could hear the neighbours working in the field behind the wall.
Farmer's children like ourselves, hungry mouths to feed,
And Spring was calling from the soil, it's time to sow the seeds.

I played beside the march ditch when I was four or five,
A thrush told all the neighbours, it's good to be alive.
The corn was shooting through the soil as we ran to and fro,
And people working in the fields, watched their children grow.

I worked beside the march ditch when I was nine or ten
Like the neighbour's children, home from school again.
But if school days seperated us because of different creeds,
Our orders now were all the same, it's time to pull the weeds.

And at seventeen the march ditch heard me sing a song
Turning hay on both sides now as the days were turning long.
We had a break in August, theirs was in July
But when one drop of rain would fall, we'd all look at the sky.

I sat beside the march ditch when I was twenty five
My heart was feeling empty as the fields before my eyes
We'd heard it on the radio another senseless death,
But when it comes so close to home it chills like winter's breath.

I look across the march ditch and every day I see
Someone on the other side who looks a lot like me.
To share this earth between us, how long does it need?
But Spring is calling from the soil, it's time to sow the seeds.

(Last line of each verse is repeated)

Newry Market

My first journey beyond the horizon of hawthorn hedges was to the local market town of Newry. A trip to Newry was a major event, you knew that you were going to a bigger place. Those who had cars would say things like, "I'll have to get her taxed some of these days, you know what they're like in the town." Those without cars travelled by foot or bicycles towards the 'broad road', the main Hilltown to Newry route. Where the Ryan Road joined the broad road you would wait for the Ulster Transport Authority's Green Bus to bring you to Newry. Other neighbours waited there as well, talking about anything and everything. The later the bus, the more news you had with you on your way to the town. An old pair, not renowned for their generosity, lived near the bus stop. One day, the male half of that pair came up the road and spiked on his unshaven chin was something which had all the appearances of soft boiled egg. When he had gone up the road a few yards, I remarked to another waiting neighbour, a woman with a nimble mind and a tongue to match, "I see Arthur must have had an egg for his breakfast this morning." "Not at all", said the woman, "it was his wife had the egg for breakfast, she just rubbed that bit onto his chin so that neighbours would think he had an egg for his breakfast."

Eventually the bus would arrive and take us on the winding road to Newry. The bus would be busiest on Thursdays and Saturdays, as people headed for Newry Market. You could buy just about anything you would want in there, and a good few things that you wouldn't want as well. Some of the salemen were pure entertainers and they knew how to hold an audience in the palm of their hands. From the hands of their audience they could also skilfully coax the red ten shilling notes and half crowns that were required to purchase their "amazing" bargains. Newry Market is there to this day even though much of its colour has been lost in the uphill struggle against shopping centres and chain stores. But it's still well worth a visit and my memories told me that it was well worth a song..

Jackson Johnston

Songs from a ceili house in the country

There was always music in our house. My earliest memories of home are associated with neighbours and relations dropping in to exchange the news of the day and to sing a few songs or play a tune or two. Everyone, from the youngest to the oldest in the company, was expected to do a turn, and even though most would make a ritual refusal at first asking, nearly everyone could eventually be coaxed into doing their party piece. The coaxing was usually lead by my father and when his own turn came round he would often sing this comical song about Jackson Johnston Jameson and I. He would always tell the assembled company how he had learned it from the Shanty McCoy, a man who he had worked with in Keenan's Scutching Mill near Mayobridge.

According to my father, the Shanty Mc Coy slept in the mill at night in a grass seed bag, a large hessian sack. The sack was suspended from a six inch nail on the wall and the Shanty slept standing up in it with his own two feet about three feet off the ground. My father wondered why he did this but he didn't like to ask, lest he might appear to be too 'forward'. And, in any case, what exercised his curiosity even more was, how did the Shanty get into that bag up on the wall. Had he a little secret ladder which he used to climb up there or, did he first get into the bag on the ground and then take a mad leap up into the air and hang himself up on the nail. My father never found out and the Shanty took the secret with him to the grave, thus leaving behind a mystery which keeps me awake at night to this day. But the Shanty also left behind the song of Jackson and Johnston. My father knew of no one other than the Shanty to sing it and I never heard it from anyone other than my father. Sometimes when I sing it, on stages thousands of miles away from that mill in Mayobridge, I think that a song is like a story or a dream - you just need one person to sing it, tell it or dream it and it will live on.

Jackson Johnston

Traditional, Arranged Colum Sands © Elm Grove Music

Sure as I went a wal- king one fine day a – long with a cou- ple of pals so gay,

There was Jack-son, John-ston, Jam-e– son and me, and oh what a jol-ly old time had we.

But we wrig-gled and we gig- gled and we laughed hee-hee, Drowning in the riv- er was the quare oul' spree,

And the people on the banks sure they laughed 'til they cried, At Jackson, Johnston, Jameson and I.

Sure as I went a walking one fine day
Along with a couple of pals so gay,
There was Jackson, Johnston, Jameson and me,
And oh what a jolly old time had we.
Now Jackson proposed we should go for a row,
So out in a jolly boat we all did go,
Well we weren't long out 'til the boat upset
And there's no need to tell you that we all got wet.

But we wriggled and we giggled and we laughed hee-hee,
Drowning in the river was the quare oul' spree,
And the people on the banks sure they laughed 'til they cried,
At Jackson, Johnston, Jameson and I.

Well they managed us ashore amidst great alarm,
We were then conveyed to a country farm,
Where they rubbed us and scrubbed us to bring us to,
And we drank hot whiskey 'til our ears turned blue.
Well we sat down together and we hung up our clothes,
In front of the fire for to dry I suppose,
Well they dried and they dried 'til they couldn't be no drier,
And the fact of the matter is our clothes caught fire.

But we wriggled and we giggled and we laughed hee-hee
Our eight- shilling suits were ablaze you see,
And wrapped up in blankets we cut a guy,
Jackson, Johnston Jameson and I.

There was nothing but our hats and our boots to be found,
The rest of our clothes they were burnt to the ground,
So we made an application to farmer John,
As we couldn't go around without our trousers on.
Now the farmer's sons were middle-sized boys,
And they wore knicky-buckers that were made of corduroys,
When we got inside of them we did look flat,
With our boots of patent leather and our tall silk hats!

But we wriggled and we giggled and we laughed hee-hee,
We were a pretty sight, the world for to see,
As we walked down the street, all the dogs did fly,
At Jackson, Johnston, Jameson and I.

Buskers

Songs from the streets of a town.

Inspiration for this song came when some of my earliest musical memories from the 1960s were brought into focus in the 1990s, after I had watched a television documentary about a cellist from Sarajevo called Vedran Smailovic. The film told the story of how Smailovic had played cello with the orchestra in Sarajevo until a bomb devastated the concert hall in that city and left the orchestra without a home. Some time later, on May 27th 1992, horror struck again when an exploding shell killed twenty two civilians as they queued for bread in the market place of Sarajevo. In the black days which followed, people were afraid to go out onto the streets and the barbaric tactic of bombing civilian targets seemed to be achieving its goal of breaking the human spirit. But Smailovic felt that he could do something to change that situation. The war had dispersed his orchestra, the concert hall was in ruins and the heart of his city had been torn out. One thing had survived though - his music. And so it happened that in the days which followed, reporters would see a strange sight and hear a haunting sound amidst the rubble of the city as Smailovic, dressed in the black suit he had once worn in the orchestra, took his cello to that spot in the market place and played there for twenty two days, one day for each life that had been lost in the bread queue.

The inspiring image of music lifting spirits in the darkest of hours caused me to think about the power of music on the streets and I found myself recalling some of the buskers that I had heard since my childhood, from Maggie Barry, the travelling singer and banjo player who used to sing outside Newry market, to 'Klaus der Geiger' playing fiddle on the streets of Cologne. I also mention the Dunne brothers from Cork in this song and, after singing it in Philadelphia one night, Mick Moloney, musicologist and lecturer in the University of New York, came out of the audience and told me that he had started to play the banjo after hearing those same Dunne brothers playing on the streets of Limerick when he was a child. It's wonderful how music and song can reach out to people and how people can step out of the verses of a song into your life. Smailovic travelled over to Ireland to play cello on a recording I was making of "Buskers" and, for a year or so after that recording, he lived in the house that had once belonged to my uncle, 'The Man with the Cap'. This song is for all the buskers and minstrels who have played and continue to play on the universal stage of the street, carrying the spirit of music across the centuries, "along the strings between the earth and the sky."

Buskers

Words & Music Colum Sands © Elm Grove Music

I saw them on the streets of Clo-nes, at a fleadh ceoil long a-go, A white-haired man with a fid-dle, his

brother had an old ban-jo, "They're blind," said the wo-man be-side us, "but by God them boys can play!" "That's the

swal-low's tail," said my fa-ther, and the mu-sic took us all a-way. And if you stop to lis-ten, they're

playing for you and I, And their music sings a-long the strings, Between the earth and the sky, Be-tween the earth and the sky....

I saw them on the streets of Clones, at a fleadh cheoil long ago,
A white-haired man with a fiddle, his brother had an old banjo,
"They're blind," said the woman beside us, "but by God them boys can play!"
"That's the swallow's tail," said my father, and the music took us all away.

Chorus
And if you stop to listen, they're playing for you and I,
And their music sings along the strings,
Between the earth and the sky,
Between the earth and the sky.

Maggie was a travelling singer, you never heard a voice so strong,
When she sang in Newry Market, the whole town heard her song,
And her voice was known from London to the streets of Baltimore,
For she sang her songs along a road that was often walked before.

Beside Cologne cathedral, a crowd had gathered round,
There was singing, there was laughing and we hurried towards the sound,
You said, "That's Klaus the fiddler, he plays here everyday,
Left the orchestra behind him, so that everyone could hear him play."

On the streets of Sarajevo, where death walks everyday,
Smailovic takes his cello and he slowly starts to play,
And the people gather round him, in the spirit of the market place,
His music brings both tears and smiles, but it changes every face.

And the music echoes all around, no matter where I stray,
Like the panpipes from the Andes, on Grafton Street today,
And some will give them money, and some will ask them why,
As the music fills the lonesome place, between the street and the sky.

Almost Every Circumstance

A song of unrequited love

This is one of my first songs and when I was writing it in my early twenties, I had already figured out that men can never understand women completely and that women never really understand men completely either. However, in the years since then, I have discovered that one of the great things in life is the challenge of trying to understand each other a little bit more each day and I'm still working on that challenge. I mentioned meeting up with Mick Moloney after singing the Buskers song one night in Philadelphia and since then I'm glad to say that we have swopped songs and yarns in many different parts of the world. Here's one of Mick's stories from life on the road and I include it here because I think it fits very well to the introduction of this song.

Mick was telling me that while he was up in Alaska one time he met a woman called Sally who informed him that in the state of Alaska there are five men to every woman. Sally lived alone but she let it be known that if she should meet the right man she might be prepared to change her single status. When Mick remarked that her chances seemed good with Alaska's population breakdown of five men to every woman, Sally came up with this wonderful reply, "Well Mick, it's like this", she said, "the odds may be good but the goods are odd." This song about the unpredictability of the odds and the goods on the pathway of human relationships is written very much from a man's viewpoint. However, if you're a woman, just turn a few words round here and there and I hope that it will make just about as much sense the other way round.

March 2000

S	M	T	W	T	F	S
			1	2	3	4
5	6	7	8	9	10	11
12	13	14	15	16	17	18
19	20	21	22	23	24	25
26	27	28	29	30	31	

Colum McEvoy 2000

Almost Every Circumstance

Words & Music Colum Sands © Elm Grove Music

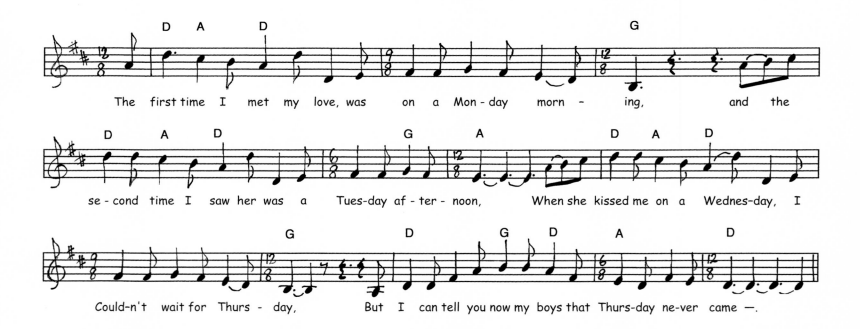

The first time I met my love, was on a Mon-day morn – ing, and the

se - cond time I saw her was a Tues-day af - ter - noon, When she kissed me on a Wednes-day, I

Could–n't wait for Thurs - day, But I can tell you now my boys that Thurs-day ne-ver came —.

The first time I met my love, was on a Monday morning,
And the second time I saw her was a Tuesday afternoon,
When she kissed me on a Wednesday, I couldn't wait for Thursday,
But I can tell you now my boys that Thursday never came.

Chorus
Seven days are in the week in almost every circumstance,
Aye, and four seasons in the year, is what we learned in school,
But never count your chickens when you're dealing with the women,
For many's the wise man fell asleep and wakened up the fool.

My love she took the Winter time and turned it into Spring time,
I never thought that love could change the world so much before,
I gave my heart and in return she promised me the summertime,
But I can tell you now my boys, that summer never came.

Whatever You Say, Say Nothing.

Do you see who's listening now?

Many of my songs are based on the expressions and turns of phrase that I have grown up with and this one draws on a phrase that is used when people are afraid to say the wrong thing in the wrong place at the wrong time. When I wrote this one I was thinking of the kind of suspicion that still lingers between the two main religious and cultural groups in my own country, for example when you'd walk into a 'mixed pub' in a place like Belfast. "Does 'mixed pub' mean a place where men and women drink?" someone once asked me in Boston and I had to clarify the situation by explaining that it's a place frequented by people who dig with both feet and therefore one where you could all too easily open your mouth and put your foot in it.

Anyway, in these mixed pubs you might find yourself looking at the person beside you over the top of your glasses - if you've got two drinks - and wondering if he's a .... And at the same time that person is also looking at you over a breast pocket full of biro pens and trying to guess if you're a .... And lest there be any confusion to the reader about this, let me assure you that I don't mean a, ... and maybe what I'm really trying to say here is that one of the main problems in this country is that no one is sure what the main problem is. Anyway, this song has been translated into a few different languages, suggesting perhaps that there's something universal in this idea of people dividing into groups and convincing themselves that they are different from the other group whether it's because of their creed, colour, nationality, the football team they support or whatever excuse they may have found. "Whatever you say, say nothing" may well be a send up on that kind of mentality, and all I can add is that if this song doesn't offend you, then I hope you won't be too offended.

Whatever you say, say nothing.

Words & Music Colum Sands © Elm Grove Music

What ev - er you say, say no - thing, when you speak a - bout you know what, For if

you know who should hear you, you know what you'll get, They'll

take you off to you know where, for you wouldn't know how long, So for

you know who's sake, don't let a – ny - one hear you sing - ing this song.

Chorus

Whatever you say, say nothing, when you speak about you know what,
For if you know who should hear you, you know what you'll get,
They'll take you off to you know where, for you wouldn't know how long,
So for you know who's sake, don't let anyone hear you singing this song.

Now you all know what I'm speaking of, when I mention you know what,
And I fear it's very dangerous, to even mention that,
For the other it is always near, although you may not see,
But if anyone asks who told you that, please don't mention me.

And you all know who I'm speaking of, when I mention you know who,
And if you know who could hear me now, you know what he'd do,
So if you don't see me again, you'll know why I'm away,
But if anyone asks you where I've gone, here's what you must say.

Well that's enough about so and so, not to mention such and such,
I'd better end my song now, I've already said too much,
For the less you say and the less you hear, the less you'll go astray,
And the less you think and the less you do, the more you'll hear them say.

The Coming of Europe

Playing ball with history.

In 1996, at the kind invitation of Ken Hudson, I crossed the Irish Sea to play my first solo concert in England. The venue was in Holmfirth, near Manchester. Two other very different events took place in Manchester on that same weekend. On the day before I arrived, a bomb wrecked the centre of the city and on the day of the concert, Sunday the 16th of June, Germany played Russia in a football match in the European Cup. For months in advance, my sons had been reminding me that the match would coincide with my concert so, needless to say, they came along. In the early afternoon we found ourselves watching the game in the awesome arena of Old Trafford. The game was a most impressive spectacle, not only for the sheer artistry and great sportsmanship on the pitch, but also for the wonderful atmosphere among the spectators around us. Russians and Germans mixed with ease, cheered together, sang together and finally exchanged congratulations and commiserations at the end of the match. It was a touching scene to witness, considering that just over fifty years earlier, these two nations had faced each other in a deadly war which had taken millions of lives from the ancestors of those players and spectators.

As I watched, my thoughts turned to the other event which had happened in Manchester that weekend and the concert which I would do that evening. That bomb from the day before had left behind not only a pile of rubble, broken glass, suffering and anger but also a reminder that not all battles are forgotten so easily among the citizens of Europe. Away back in 1690, a Dutch prince and a Scottish King battled for the Crown of England. Who could have predicted that the memories of that battle would still hold bitterness three hundred years later? And then again, who could have predicted the scenes on the terraces at that football match? Perhaps one way to disperse bitterness is to view the scene from a different window and a slightly different angle. As European borders came tumbling down in the early 1990s, I wrote this song with a view to changing the view that has been etched in the memory for three centuries, long after the sound of the final whistle. "Three hundred years is a long time to learn but I hope we can learn all the same, That most people lose when their country is used for dangerous military games."

REMEMBER 1690
WHAT ABOUT 1992?
HERE WE GO HERE WE GO
HERE WE GO
COLUM McEVOY '89.

The Coming of Europe

Words & music Colum Sands © Elm Grove Music

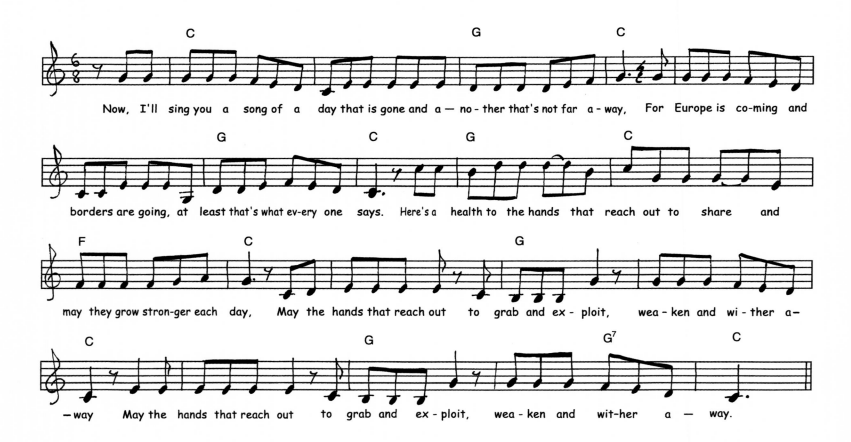

Now, I'll sing you a song of a day that is gone and a — no - ther that's not far a - way, For Europe is co-ming and

borders are going, at least that's what ev-ery one says. Here's a health to the hands that reach out to share and

may they grow stron-ger each day, May the hands that reach out to grab and ex - ploit, wea — ken and wi - ther a—

—way May the hands that reach out to grab and ex - ploit, wea - ken and wit-her a — way.

I'll sing you a song of a day that is gone and another that's not far away,
For Europe is coming and borders are going, at least that's what everyone says.
Here's a health to the hands that reach out to share and may they grow stronger each day,
May the hands that reach out to grab and exploit, weaken and wither away.

Now it wasn't the day nor the day before that, when Europe gave us a surprise,
A big international was due to be played with the crown of oul' England as prize.
Scotland and Holland were into the final and no tougher teams could be found,
So somebody said, in the interests of peace, they should play in a neutral ground.

First Rome was suggested but that was contested for reasons that I can't explain,
But it seems every country was awfully shy about hosting the crowd pulling game.
'Til a brain waving diplomat stuck up his hand, saying I know a field that is fine,
It's lovely and flat and there's room for a crowd and it lies on the banks of the Boyne.

Well the venue decided, the date it was set, and training was soon underway,
As Europe prepared for the game of the year in the more-or-less usual way.
Flags were brought out and excursions arranged, a charter from France was the plan,
As the Irish prepared to play host to a game that would change every woman and man.

When the day of the final at last came along, excitement had risen so much,
That over in Rome they were praying all day, that victory would go to the Dutch.
Now it seems that the stewarts were thin on the ground, spectators were soon out of hand,
The Irish took sides and the battle it raged 'til it ravished the half of the land.

Now the Dutch won the cup and both teams disappeared leaving death and destruction behind,
And so much ill feeling that three hundred years could not put it out of our minds.
Now three hundred years is a long time to learn but I hope we can learn all the same,
That most people lose when their country is used, for dangerous military games.

(Repeat first verse)

Goethe's Song

A love song from Germany

"We ought, everyday at least to hear a little song, read a good poem, see a fine picture, and if it were possible, to speak a few reasonable words." — Goethe.

Had Johann Wolfgang von Goethe been an historian rather than a poet, his writing might have been fuelled by the far reaching changes he witnessed in his lifetime. Between his birth in Frankfurt in 1749 and his death in Weimar in 1832 he saw great upheavals in society, from the vast transformation in living conditions to the radical changes which took place in the sciences and the arts. All of this happened in a lifetime that spanned the Seven Years War, the rise and fall of Napoleon, and the American and French Revolutions. Fortunately, his writing followed another path and he turned out some of the greatest works in German and world literature. Of his work he once said, "I shaped only what I felt, what burned in my heart." This may well be the reason why his work is of universal appeal, reaching across time and place and shortening the autobahns of Germany for a man born on the Ryan Road near Mayobridge some two hundred years later.

It seems that Goethe's most famous work, Faust, burned in his heart for sixty years before he finally declared it complete on the year before his death. Gretchen, the heroine of that work, was also the name of his first love. She appeared in his life when he was fifteen and, in the years which followed, there would be more women to attract and inspire, until at the age of seventy three, he declared his love for the seventeen year old Ulrike von Levetzow, remembered in his Elegy of Marienbad. It has been said that Goethe felt and sang for each one of his loves as though it were the last and only love of his life. That certainly holds true in his poem, Naehe des Geliebten, a poem which reminded me that there are few people who have not experienced the feeling of being at a distance from someone who is close to their hearts. In attempting to translate and set it to music, I soon realised that there are few writers who could equal Goethe in capturing the heart and soul of that feeling.

I will say no more by way of explanation, remembering Goethe's own words "I am the enemy of long explanations; they deceive either the maker or the hearer, generally both."

Goethe's Song

Original German by Goethe, English Translation and Music Colum Sands © Elm Grove Music

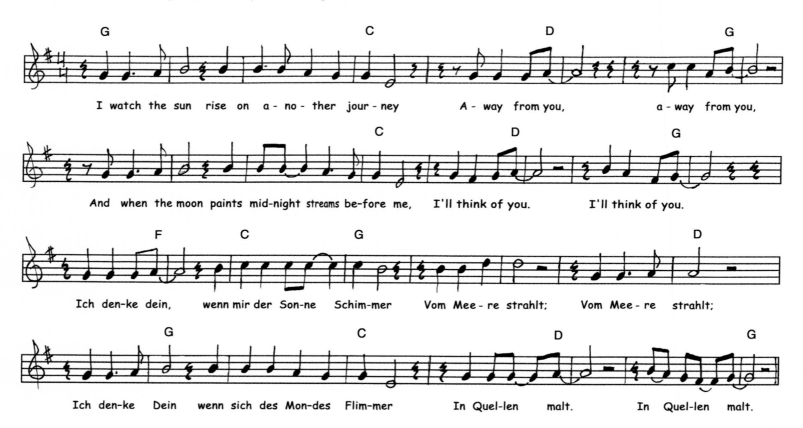

I watch the sun rise on a - no - ther jour - ney A - way from you, a - way from you,

And when the moon paints mid-night streams be-fore me, I'll think of you. I'll think of you.

Ich den-ke dein, wenn mir der Son-ne Schim-mer Vom Mee - re strahlt; Vom Mee - re strahlt;

Ich den-ke Dein wenn sich des Mon-des Flim-mer In Quel-len malt. In Quel-len malt.

I watch the sun rise on another journey
Away from you, away from you,
And when the moon paints midnight streams before me,
I'll think of you, I'll think of you.

Ich denke dein, wenn mir der Sonne Schimmer
Vom Meere strahlt;
Ich denke dein wenn sich des Mondes Flimmer
In Quellen malt, In Quellen malt.

And I see you on every road I travel,
On the laughing street and down the lonely mile,
Through the darkest nights of all my winding journeys,
I see your smile, I see your smile.

Ich sehe dich, wenn auf dem fernen Wege,
Der Staub sich hebt;
In tiefer Nacht, wenn auf dem schmalen Stege
Der Wandrer bebt, Der Wandrer bebt.

I hear your voice from the rustling leaves of morning,
Til the winds of evening knock my window pane,
And in the silence of the deepest forest,
I hear your name, I hear your name.

Ich hoere dich, wenn dort mit dumpfem Rauschen
Die Welle steight
Im stillen Haine gehe ich oft so lauschen
Wenn alles schweight, Wenn alles schweight.

You're by my side, though distance stands between us,
I know you're near, I know you're near
The sun goes down but the stars will walk beside us,
Til you are here, til you are here.

Ich bin bei dir, du seist auch noch so ferne,
Du bist mir nah!
Die Sonne sinkt, bald leuchten mir die Sterne,
O waerst du da, O waerst du da!

I'm a Terrible Man

On the subject of translations

A few days ago, in May 2000, I was speaking to a woman from Leeds who had just started work in Chester and she was telling me that people there were continually teasing her about her accent. "And the strange thing is", she said, "I didn't have any accent at all until I left home." I knew what she meant and indeed I have to say that I really enjoy listening to all the different accents and versions of English that are to be found around the world. The English used in and around home is an interesting blend of Elizabethan English, the gaelic languages of Ireland and Scotland and many other bits and pieces as well. It can be confusing for the visitor and if ever a comprehensive book of phrases comes along to help clear this confusion, let me suggest a title, The Royal Ulster Vocabulary.

Although that woman I mentioned had no accent until she left home, I was already beginning to enjoy local words and turns of phrase from an early age on the road where I grew up. The Ryan Road was fairly quiet traffic wise and I've already mentioned that one of the few vehicles on the road was Jimmy Mc Gowan's multi purpose bread van which brought everything from 'paris buns' and plain loaves to newspapers and wet batteries. A woman called Martha lived just up the road from us and she kept a cat called Big Bun which I think may have been supplied by the breadman as well. Anyway, Big Bun had figured out the local pace of life and used to sleep in the middle of the road, knowing that there wouldn't be much traffic to contend with. One morning, as I was walking past Martha's house on the way to school, the bread van appeared on an unscheduled flight, one day earlier than usual, and indeed neighbours talked about it for months afterwards. Big Bun was sleeping in the middle of the road as usual and the bread van came hurtling round the corner at about five miles an hour. At the very last second, with a wrench of the steering wheel and a sigh rather than a screech of tyres, the breadman and his van managed to miss the sleeping cat by a whisker. Martha, who had witnessed the lucky escape through her kitchen window, came out of the house dusting flour off her hands and said to me as she pointed at Big Bun, "You know if that cat had been a dog, it would have been a dead duck." Looking back now, I think that these are the twists of dialect and turns of phrase which lead us down those fascinating byroads that avoid the straight boring motorways of perfect grammar. Long may the spoken word keep these roads alive, whether we leave home or not.

I'm a Terrible Man

Words & music Colum Sands © Elm Grove Music

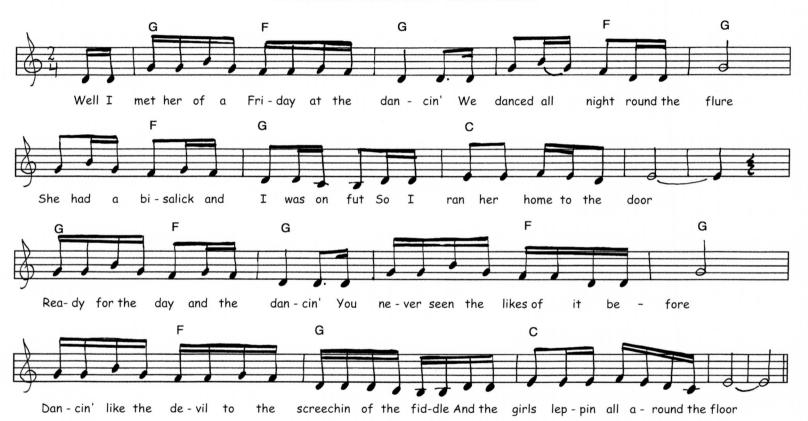

Well I met her of a Fri-day at the dan-cin' We danced all night round the flure

She had a bi-salick and I was on fut So I ran her home to the door

Rea-dy for the day and the dan-cin' You ne-ver seen the likes of it be - fore

Dan-cin' like the de-vil to the screechin of the fid-dle And the girls lep-pin all a - round the floor

Well I met her of a Friday at the dancin'
We danced all night round the flure
She had a bisalick and I was on fut
So I ran her home to the door

Chorus
Ready for the day and the dancin'
You never seen the likes of it before
Dancin' like the devil to the screechin of the fiddle
And the girls lepin' all around the floor

"Come on on in, you boy yeh,
We can't stand out in the coul'
There's no one at home barren daddy
And he be to be sleepin' by now"

She gave me a rake of biscakes
And a cupful of tae in my hand
When I heard a kind of phistle in a back o' me
It was daddy, and he was some man!

Her father he let out a gulder
You talk about getting' a gunk,
But I duked in around by the jaw box
And I dunted him into the bunk

She was a whinging and a gernin'
And he was roarin' on the flure
If I catch a hoult of your thrapple
But I was headin' for the door

I ran through the nettles and the gutters
I wish that I had took a luk
For I jumped through a hedge and I landed
Up to my oxsters in a sheugh

But I'll go back to see her
Her father can do what he can
And I'll go back to the dancin'
For I'm a terrible man!

Lookin' the Loan of a Spade

Learning to understand what's not said.

One of the great things about travelling is that you learn to see yourself through other people's eyes and in this way you discover things that you'd never have noticed about yourself had you stayed at home in the first place. I wouldn't have written this song had I not journeyed to places like Germany where people are much more direct about coming to the point than we are at home. I was made aware of this on my very first trip there in 1973 when the woman of a house near Muenster asked me if I'd like a cup of tea. Needless to say I observed the Irish custom of saying "No thanks" and to my consternation, I didn't get a cup of tea. This came as a great shock to me because in Ireland (and in Norway also, as I discovered just a few months ago) you always say "no thanks" first. The ritual then goes, "Are you sure now you wouldn't like a cup of tea?" to which you reply, "No, no, I don't want to put you to any trouble." This, by the way, is the first sign of weakness. "No trouble at all, I'm making a cup of tea anyway" is the next offer, which then gives you the opening to complete the cycle with words like, "Well if you're making a cup of tea anyway, I'll take a cup of tea."

I'm fascinated by these rituals where the words used are not to be taken at their face value. Indeed it's almost as if they're merely sounds which are being thrown around and exchanged in a seemingly random way to test, probe and move a little bit closer to the other person. In Japan, for example, you would be ill advised to go to someone's home when invited there. Apparently the ritual in Japan requires that you be invited three times and only when you've been invited for the third time can you assume that the invitation is there to be accepted - not unlike the tea ritual in Ireland. For many years I had been thinking of a way to hoard these circuitous routes of communication into the verses of a song and my search stopped when I remembered situations at home many years ago when we'd be sent to borrow things from the neighbours. On those occasions, the last thing you'd want to talk about to your neighbour was the thing you had come to borrow and so, this song about borrowing a spade emerged, laden with all those sounds that are used when we are testing, probing and generally educating each other in the great skill of reading between the lines of life.

Lookin' the loan of a Spade

Words & music Colum Sands © Elm Grove Music

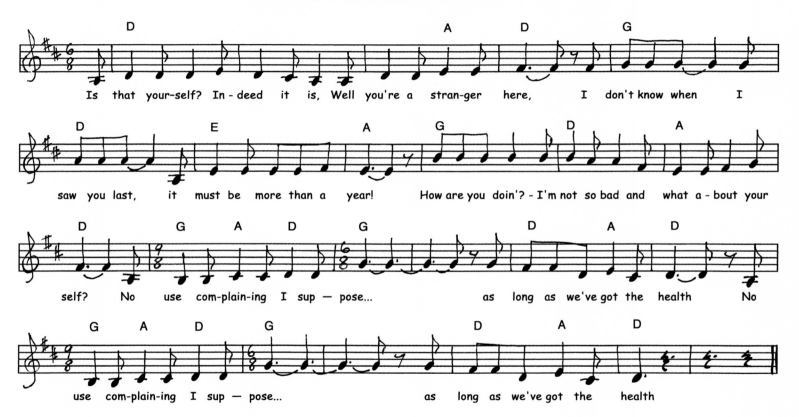

Is that your–self? In - deed it is, Well you're a stran-ger here, I don't know when I

saw you last, it must be more than a year! How are you doin'? - I'm not so bad and what a - bout your

self? No use com-plain-ing I sup — pose... as long as we've got the health No

use com-plain-ing I sup — pose... as long as we've got the health

Is that yourself? -Indeed it is - Well you're a stranger here,
I don't when I seen you last, it must be more than a year!
How are you doing? - I'm not so bad and what about yourself?
-No use complaining I suppose as long as we've got the health.

-Where are you now? - I'm still at home, it's the brother that went away,
My father said that if one of us left, the other would have to stay,
Sure jobs are getting very scarce, the unemployment's a curse,
-But still I suppose as the fella says, it's bad that couldn't be worse.

-Terrible weather altogether, it's never going to clear!
-Do you know what I'm going to tell you though, it's not bad for the time of the year,
Sure a sup of rain never done very much harm, the grass could do with a drop,
I'd pass no remarks on a skift or two, as long as there's not a slap.

-Aye a slap's the last thing that we need, for our wee meadow's in hay,
Do you mind the trade we had last year coming up thon bit of a brae?
-The mountain's coming very close, I don't like the look of the sky,
The forecast talked about a change, but you mightn't believe thon boys.

-I suppose I'd better be headin' on, I've held you back enough,
I was clearing up at the back of the house, the garden is very rough,
I broke the spade and it's awkward, when you've only got a graip,
And unless I can get the loan of a spade, the garden will have to wait.

-Aye a spade's an awful missly thing, there's the sun again,
But it's only a pet it'll never keep up, I felt a spit of rain,
-Would you be using your spade today? - To tell you the truth I'm not,
For I lent it to you a year ago, and since then I never saw it.

I'm the King of the Castle

Remembering a children's song

Sometimes a look back down the road to childhood can yield an idea for a story or a song and I'll start off with a story. Along with my brothers and sisters I walked a few miles to school each day and we were always expected to bring some news home with us. Neighbours along the way would often ask us if we had any news from home or school, they in turn would pass on their news to us and we would eventually arrive home with at least the main headlines of the day. In this way neighbours were well informed about each other - a contrast to the news system of today where we know what is happening on the other side of the world but have no idea about how well our next door neighbours might be. I remember one September afternoon, arriving home with my younger brother Eugene who at the age of four had just started school. Our father met us as we were coming down the lane to the house and asked us, "Well, any news at school today?" "Yes", said my brother Eugene, remembering something he had seen at a house on the way from school, "I have some news, Paddy Mullan has a new pony." "And what colour is the pony?" my father wanted to know. Eugene applied his four year old mind to this question for a few seconds and then replied, "I don't know. I couldn't see what colour it was because the pony was all covered with hair."

There's a kind of childlike logic in that reply and I hope there is something similar in this song. "I'm the king of the castle and you're the dirty wee rascal" is a children's play rhyme, usually sung or chanted by the child who, for a few seconds at least, has climbed higher than the others. The chanting sounds of superiority don't always end with childhood and indeed it seems that rulers have always ebbed and flowed with the tide of history, coming and going, each climbing and clambering over the shoulders of the less fortunate until, for a glimpse in time, they can take their turn to crow at the top of the hill.

MR.KING

COLUM McEVOY 2000.

The King of the Castle

Words & Music Colum Sands © Elm Grove Music

Well there was a lit-tle king and he was a lit-tle ras-cal-o First he built a house and then he built a castle-o At

least he gave the or-ders to all his lit-tle wor-kers-o He sat on his throne, a sip ping his red wine - o. Sayin'

I am the king of the cas-tle-o and you are the dir-ty wee ras - cal - o and

I am the king of the cas-tle-o and you are the dir-ty wee ras - cal - o

Well there was a little king and he was a little rascal-o
First he built a house and then he built a castle-o
At least he gave the orders to all his little workers-o
He sat on his throne, a sipping his red wine-o.

Chorus
Sayin' I am the king of the castle-o
And you are the dirty wee rascal-o
I am the king of the castle-o
And you are the dirty wee rascal-o

Well the castle it grew bigger and the workers they grew smaller-o
The more the king grew fat, the more he gave his orders-o
Until the job was done and he threw a big party-o
Invited all his friends but none of them were workers-o

Well the feast went on for hours and everyone grew fatter-o
But still they gorged themselves, for that was in their nature-o
Until there was a bang that was heard for miles around-o
The castle fell to pieces like a castle built of sand-o

Now there's some say the bang was caused by the workers-o,
Some say it was stomachs that could simply hold no more-o
And others say they fear that there always will be bangs-o
As long as some eat all, while others must go hungry-o

One of these days

Finding the time

If you ever take a drive around the shores of Strangford Lough in County Down you should pay a visit to the monastery of Nendrum on Mahee Island. It's in an area that was once home to one of Europe's great centres of learning, but today, trees and birds are more likely to provide the company than humans, scholarly or otherwise. Time will have its way with most man made structures but as you look at the few walls of the monastery which remain, you should know that these well-worn stones contain the spirit of a wonderful story about time, the story of a monk called Mochaoi. He lived in Nendrum monastery in the latter part of the 6th century AD and, according to a story that survives from medieval texts, he left the monastery one day to go out into the forest. Before he had walked very far, his attention was taken by the most beautiful music he had ever heard. It was the sound of a bird singing in the trees, some distance away, and it sang three different strains, each one more enchanting than the one before. Mochaoi stopped and listened in awe. Time stood still to listen as well and it seemed as if that bird song was the only sound in the whole world. At last, as the sound faded and the daylight faded too, a great tiredness came over Mochaoi and he made his way back to the monastery with heavy feet. To his surprise, he didn't recognise the first monk he met at the door nor the second and the third was still more of a stranger to him. Worse still, they didn't know who he was either. Eventually a very old monk came hobbling up and whispered that he remembered an even older monk telling him about an entry in the annals of Nendrum relating to a monk of that name who had disappeared. They turned back the faded pages of that book and there, sure enough, they found a few lines about a monk called Mochaoi who had gone into the forest one hundred and fifty years earlier and never returned.

Similar stories of time frozen are to be found throughout Europe and I think that in a certain way, their message may have inspired this song. In spite of our best intentions, we can find ourselves at the end of school days, careers or relationships wondering what happened to the past ten, twenty or fifty years. There may be more time saving devices around now than there were when Mochaoi lived in Nendrum but yet, to this very day it seems that we still don't have enough time.

One of these days

Words & Music Colum Sands © Elm Grove Music

Look - ing through an old school at - las, I found your pho - to once a - gain sand is fal - ling

through your fin - gers as you smile in - to the lens. One of these days we'll get to-geth-er,

one of these days we'll take the time, One of these days we'll get to geth-er, right back to the star-ting line.

Looking through an old school atlas, I found your photo once again
The sand is falling through your fingers as you smile into the lens.

Chorus
One of these days we'll get together, one of these days we'll take the time,
One of these days we'll get together, right back to the starting line.

Met you at the busy corner, hardly time to say hello,
I'm in the phone book, call me sometime, sorry now I'll have to go.

I hear you're married, how's it going, son and daughter just like me,
Before you know it, school and homework, must go now it's nearly three.

Dreamt last night that we were running, once again along the strand,
School days over, we were writing, good intentions in the sand.

Traffic lights arranged this meeting, who's that man beside you now..
Your son? he's seventeen already, lights turned green, I'll have to fly.

Met your son at the busy corner, heard the news and shook his hand,
But still you smile out from the photo, as the sand falls through your hands..

Directions

Finding the way

To follow a song about being lost in time, here's one about getting lost in place. We have already learned that no one has an accent until they leave home and I suppose, in the same way, no one will ever get lost until they leave the territory that is familiar to them. There's a story told about a child asking a shepherd why he stands out on the cold mountain all day and sometimes all night too. The shepherd explains that he has to look after the sheep in case they might get lost. The child looks towards the sheep as they wander around nibbling at the grass contentedly and then asks, "And would a sheep know that it was lost?" I know that I am lost when I've driven around in circles for an hour or so and find myself taking the ultimate measure of stopping to ask for directions. It's a tricky thing to do in any country and in most places you'll find that ninety per cent of the people you ask don't actually live there themselves. The other ten per cent, feeling the power of having knowledge that you don't have, will take great delight in telling you things like "you couldn't be further wrong, what took you this way?" or "you're away off your road altogether!" And so on and so on, I know variations of those phrases in several languages now. Others will give you coded messages like the mechanic in Aughnacloy who was attending to an old car of mine many years ago when I was on my way to Donegal. "Is there anywhere here where I could get something to eat while you're fixing the car?" I asked him. He thought for a few seconds, changed the spanner from one hand to the other and then replied, "Yes, there are two places here where you could get a bite to eat." "And which one would you recommend?" I wanted to know. He considered this question, returned the spanner to the hand it had been in earlier and then confided, "Well it's like this, no matter which one you go to, when you come out, you'll wish you had gone to the other one." So you need to have your wits about you when you ask directions anywhere and this song is a collection of advice that has been delivered through the rolled down window of enquiry over all those years and miles that make up the curriculum of the University of Life.

Directions

Words & Music Colum Sands © Elm Grove Music

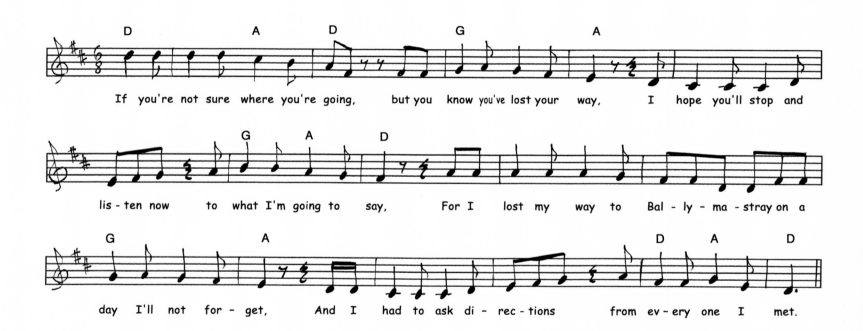

If you're not sure where you're going, but you know you've lost your way, I hope you'll stop and lis-ten now to what I'm going to say, For I lost my way to Bal-ly–ma-stray on a day I'll not for–get, And I had to ask di–rec-tions from ev–ery one I met.

If you're not sure where you're going, but you know you've lost your way,
I hope you'll stop and listen now to what I'm going to say,
For I lost my way to Ballymastray on a day I'll not forget,
And I had to ask directions from everyone I met.
Well my trouble really started at the crossroads I suppose,
When I asked a man coming out of a shop with smoke coming out of his nose,
He leaned in through my window, like a man with time to spare,
And through the smoke I heard him say, "Now you're a stranger here.

But do you see that road in front of you that's forking to the right,
Whatever you do, don't take that road or you'll drive about all night,
No just you keep on going, til you see a pub called Pat's,
Drive straight on round the corner and ask anyone after that."
Well round the bend I drove myself and I didn't see a soul,
Til I met a man with a bicycle he was wheeling a bag of coal,
His face was slightly swollen and his back wheel slightly flat,
But I knew I'd have to ask him, I was lost and that was that.

"Could you tell me the way to Ballymastray?" - "Could you give us the price of a beer?"
I handed him over a couple of bob for I thought the deal was fair,
Til his pickled words of wisdom were whispered in my ear,
"If I was going to Ballymastray, I wouldn't start from here."
A woman tied to a little dog next heard my appeal,
As she leaned through my window, her dog leaned on my wheel,
"O Ballymastray's a lovely place, sure it's even in a song,
But do you know what I'm going to tell you though, you couldn't be further wrong!

You see, you came across the river, and you really had no call,
In fact you shouldn't have crossed that bridge at all at all at all.."
Her dog had reached my fourth wheel as I put the car in gear,
Says I, " I'm getting out of here before he finds the spare."
It was just outside a joke shop, I met a man with a gun,
Black polish painted on his face and he wore a uniform,
I asked for the way to Ballymastray, says he, "I'm not from here"
He asked me where I was coming from, says I "I've no idea!"

Ah, never ask a couple, unless you want a fight,
One will send you to the left and the other to the right,
I left a pair at loggerheads and then my blood ran cold,
For wheeling round the corner came the man with the bag of coal.
"Ah now you're really lost my boy, and there's just yourself to blame,
For you drove away the minute I was trying to explain,
But I'll tell you now for nothing, if you take me and my load,
I'll show you the way to Ballymastray and it won't be off your road."

It was half an hour later, we reached his granny's lane,
And there we left his bag of coal and headed on again,
He left me with directions an hour after that,
At a petrol pump with a pub attached and the name of the pub was Pat's.
When I reached my destination, I was a broken man,
But the lesson that I learned that day, I'll share it if I can,
If you're going to Ballyshannon, Ballymastray or Ballylap,
If you're going to Bally anywhere, would you buy a bally map.

The Marching Season

Finding a solution, in a dream.

It was a beautiful evening in July 1988. The town was ablaze with all the colours of summer, a blue sky looking down on sun-browned skins as the greenery of trees and plants provided a lush backdrop for the wild reds and yellows of flowers in the window boxes along either side of the street. I couldn't tell you the names of those flowers, I didn't recognise many of them and I didn't care, they looked so good that it didn't seem to matter what they were called in any language. The scent of summer was in the air too, that sense of warmth that rises out of the streets and pavements, promising that some heat will linger on, long after the sun has disappeared. I had a feeling that this festival would continue regardless of the time of day or night but, for now, the sun was right up there above us, inviting everyone to celebrate the summer. I squinted in the bright light and looked down the street. The sound of cheering arose as a band blared into view, surrounded by dancers, jugglers and all kinds of street entertainers. They were dressed in strange medieval costumes and, as I glanced up at the colourful canopy of banners and bunting which floated above their heads, I became aware that I didn't recognise any of the flags and noted at the same time that, for some reason or other, I didn't really care. A young dark haired woman trailed slightly behind the main group, her brown arms wrapped around a curious looking stringed instrument. It looked vaguely familiar - perhaps I had seen one in an old painting or book once - but I couldn't have put a name on it. The woman was a complete stranger to me but then, so too was everyone else in this town of San Sebastian de los Reyes. Nevertheless, she seemed to have detached herself from the main group of musicians and dancers and was walking towards me now with what might have been a question forming on her lips. I found myself wondering whether we spoke the same language and, if we did, what we might talk about. I could ask her what her name was, find out the names of those flowers, what that strange musical instrument was called or, perhaps I could inquire about the meaning of the flags and banners in that parade which was now fast fading out of view. However, before either of us could speak, a new sound suddenly filled the space that had been left behind by the band. It was a voice and accent from home, bringing me up to date with the very latest news there. "I see things are looking rough again for the Marching Season, 1690 and all that, you know what I mean?" Much later that night I woke up and wrote this song.

The Marching Season

Words & Music Colum Sands ¬© Elm Grove Music

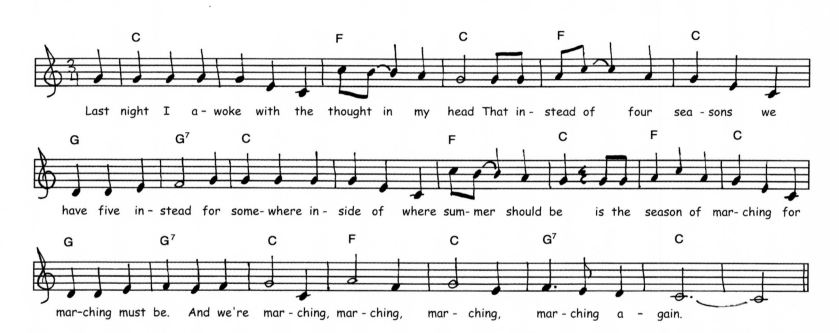

Last night I a-woke with the thought in my head That in-stead of four sea-sons we

have five in-stead for some-where in-side of where sum-mer should be is the season of mar-ching for

mar-ching must be. And we're mar-ching, mar-ching, mar-ching, mar-ching a-gain.

Last night I awoke with the thought in my head
That instead of four seasons we have five instead
For somewhere inside of where summer should be
Is the season of marching for marching must be.

Chorus
And we're marching, marching, marching, marching again.

Now four of the seasons give forecasters pain,
Will it be sunshine or will it be rain?
Leinster say thunder and Connaught say blow
Munster say hailstones and Ulster say snow.

But each year the fifth season's easily forecast,
Don't look at the weather map look at the past,
Temperatures high and tolerance low,
If you've somewhere to go it's the right time to go.

Then I says to myself if marching must be,
Let's do the thing right so the whole world can see,
We'll build a big stadium centrally placed,
With a circular route where the marchers can pace.

To build such a place would throw lots of the dole,
Stones could be thrown in a meaningful role,
As builders and masons regardless of creed,
Build the big marching stadium we so badly need.

There's be seating for tourists to sit and to stare,
In our wonderful heritage they'd have a share,
And a fiver a seat isn't money in vain,
To travel three centuries down memory lane.

Riot facilities would be provided,
Dressing rooms could be hired mixed or divided,
And to really pull in massive crowds we could hope,
For annual concerts by Queen and the Pope.

Then marchers could march all the whole year around,
No longer the trouble of marching through towns
Safe in the stadium the glorious past,
While the rest of us turn to the present at last.

Good Friday Never Changes

Thoughts at a train station

Airports and train stations are places where great energy circles are created by the exchanges of those who are travelling and those who are staying behind. I've been in those places many times but I know that I will never become sufficiently travel-hardened to remain unmoved by the sight of people rushing forward to greet each other and those who are reluctantly saying goodbye. Without really wanting to, I often find myself observing those who have just taken their leave and are preparing to travel onwards alone. A change takes place, and I know this from my own experience as well. The sadness of parting may linger for minutes or hours but eventually you acknowledge that you're really alone now and it's time to draw upon your own strength for the next stage of the journey. Some of that strength comes from those left behind or those who are waiting further along the track and part of it may come from a place that's not on any train timetable. Travelling alone can be one way of finding time to think about that place or space or whatever you may want to call it and such thoughts were in my mind during one of those long train journeys across Germany in 1977. There is a relentlessness about the sound of a train that plays tricks with my perception of time and even place as well. As the wine valleys of the Rhine flashed past the window, I found myself comparing the train journey with the passage of life itself and thinking how, whether we realise it or not, we are constantly moving towards or away from those we know and those we have yet to meet. Somewhere between those places of parting and meeting on that Good Friday, this song arrived as the train sped along on its endless journey onwards.

Colum McEvoy 2000.

Good Friday never changes

Words & Music Colum Sands ¬© Elm Grove Music

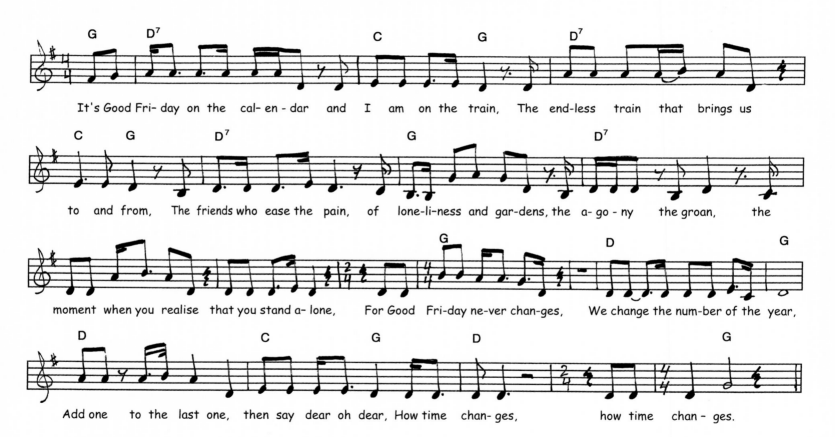

It's Good Friday on the calendar and I'm on the train,
The endless train that brings us to and from,
The friends who ease the pain, of loneliness in gardens, the agony, the groan,
The moment when you realise that you stand alone,

Chorus
For Good Friday never changes,
We change the number of the year,
Add one to the last one, then say dear o dear,
How time changes, how time changes.

Were you the one who tried to change the evil that you found,
Or did you stand uncertain at the edge of the crowd,
As he was led away, you didn't raise the hand, that once had flung the palm,
In the waters of indifference, you stooped to wash your hands,

And now we've reached the station, see how the people run,
Laughing and crying, to and from,
The friends who ease the pain, of loneliness in gardens, the agony, the groan,
The moment when you realise that you stand alone.

Long Road to Perfection.

The price of progress

It seems that for every potentially beneficial invention and discovery that comes along in the course of history, someone finds a way to turn it against the well being of humanity. This can be traced from the stone age to the middle ages, then on to the transformation of an agrarian society by the industrial revolution and right through to the present day when we've reached the stage where many of the more powerful "civilised" countries have economies that are largely dependent on their arms industries. In his book "Hidden Agendas" John Pilger traces the beginnings of the modern arms trade to the 1860s when a Newcastle upon Tyne lawyer called William Armstrong set up in competition with the German arms manufacturer Alfred Krupp. By the 1880s there was more competition in the ring as the Sheffield based Vickers brothers joined the game with their highly successful machine-gun invented by Sir Hiram Maxim.

In 1905, Vickers paid £86,000 to their chief salesman Sir Basil Zaharoff, and on his way to becoming a millionaire that particular knight showed that he understood the game just as well as many of the more powerful people around in today's world. "I made wars so that I could sell arms to both sides," he boasted. "I must have sold more arms than anyone else in the world." The game continues and, just a few years ago, the on going madness and hypocrisy was captured within two separate articles sharing the front page of the Guardian newspaper. One described how the Queen knelt as shops fell silent around the country for the school children who had died in the massacre of Dunblane, the other described the involvement of GEC in an arms deal worth £5 billion in the Middle East. It would be easy to allow such a scenario to cover us in clouds of pessimism but I believe that things can be changed through the strength and conviction of those who are working today to build a peaceful future.

"It can't be done, it won't be done, I've tried it all before,"
Says weary faced Experience, closing up the door.
And yet I'll try it one more time, a fool though I may seem
The world must be surprised each day, by those who dare to dream.

Long Road to Perfection

Words & Music Colum Sands ¬© Elm Grove Music

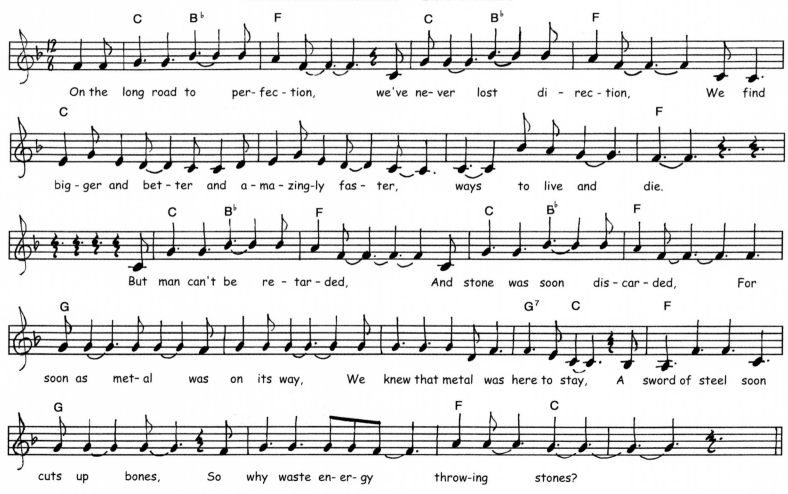

On the long road to per-fec-tion, we've ne-ver lost di – rec-tion, We find

big-ger and bet–ter and a-ma-zing-ly fas–ter, ways to live and die.

But man can't be re – tar-ded, And stone was soon dis-car-ded, For

soon as met-al was on its way, We knew that metal was here to stay, A sword of steel soon

cuts up bones, So why waste en-er-gy throw-ing stones?

In days of stone the cavemen,
Ate raw meat without sauce on,
'Til a genius found a flint stone,
And fire was soon the fashion,
For heating and cooking, or even rebuking,
People you couldn't rely on.

Chorus
On the long road to perfection,
We've never lost direction,
We find bigger and better and amazingly faster,
Ways to live and die.

But man can't be retarded,
And stone was soon discarded,
For as soon as metal was on its way,
We knew that metal was here to stay,
A sword of steel soon cuts up bones,
So why waste energy throwing stones?

The day of the savages drifted by,
Towns and cities leaped to the sky
We built factories over the land,
Machines saved muscles though they claimed some hands
And if at times our health declined,
Production was faster so we didn't really mind..

Communication by road and rail,
Radio and air outdated the sail
Let's be faster the inventors cried,
But between ourselves communication died,
And the gadgets we made with all our skill
Included little gadgets that would kill, kill, kill

On the road to perfection we've reached the stage
Of nuclear power the atomic age
We've reached the moon and next is Mars
And we've found a way to end all wars,
But for every forward step we make,
We always seem to take two back..

Blame the World

Don't blame me...

In the village of Rostrevor, where I live, a little river flows through the magical leafy glade which is known as the Fairy Glen. That name alone suggests some connection with another world and indeed, if you want to transport yourself a few steps away from the rush of today's world, the Fairy Glen is the place to go for a stroll. As you walk out of the village, the little river tumbles down through the trees from the hills above and makes its way into Carlingford Lough. Rostrevor, nestling on the shores of that lough looks across the water towards Sliabh Foy and the Cooley Peninsula, pointing the way towards The Irish Sea. It's an idyllic place at any time of the year and just a few weeks ago I came to see it in another way. I had just finished reading a book about Native American Indians, and words from those pages came floating back to me when I noticed a couple of plastic bags and beer cans drifting downstream.

I had learned from the book how Mato-Kuwapi, a Santee-Yanktonai Sioux had spoken just before his death in 1915 about the importance of the sun dance to his tribe. His words also showed the deep understanding which his people had for the balance of nature and, that day as I watched the river flowing towards the sadly polluted Irish Sea, I couldn't help thinking how much we have to learn about that balance. Here is what Mato-Kuwapi said, "When a man does a piece of work which is admired by all we say that it is wonderful; but when we see the changes of day and night, the sun, moon, and stars in the sky, and the changing seasons upon the earth, with their ripening fruits, anyone must realise that it is the work of some one more powerful than man. Greatest of all is the sun, without which we cannot live,"

A few years ago, in the sunshine of the Fiddlers Green International Festival in Rostrevor, a group of children began what has now become an annual event by cleaning up the rubbish along the river. Assisted by local conservationists and folksingers like the late Danny Kyle from Scotland, their example inspired us all and prompted the local angling club to restock the waters of the river with fish. And, by a lovely turn of the cycle, after one of those clean-ups, the children were entertained by a musician called Sky Walking Stick Man Alone, a member of the Choctaw tribe. Initiatives like these may seem small but nevertheless, in direct contrast to the indifference which is pointed out in 'Blame the World', they are a beginning. And beginnings such as these grow up to bring about real change through action, regardless of whether that action is inspired by our children or the ancient wisdom that came before us.

Blame the World

Words & Music Colum Sands ¬© Elm Grove Music

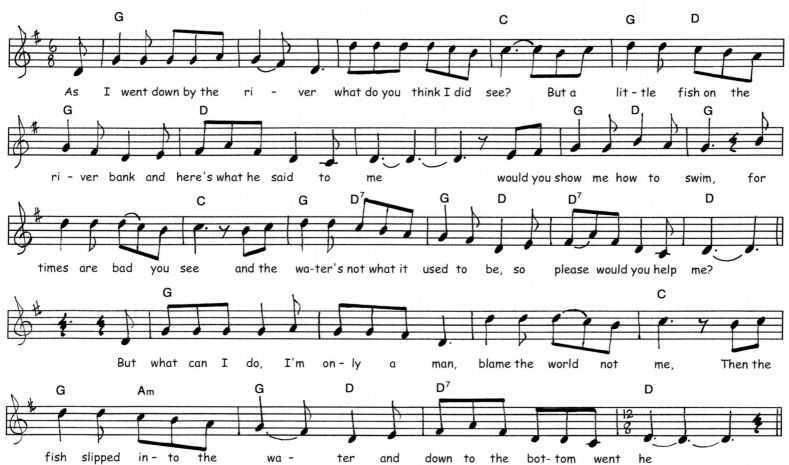

As I went down by the river, what do you think I did see?
But a little fish on the river bank and here's what he said to me –
Would you show me how to swim, for times are bad you see
And the water's not what it used to be, so please would you help me?

– But what can I do, I'm only a man, blame the world not me,
Then the fish slipped into the water and down to the bottom went he.

As I went over the meadow, what do you think I did see?
But a blackbird hanging onto a branch, and here's what she said to me-
Would you show me how to fly, for times are bad you see,
And the air is not what it used to be, so please could you help me?

– But what can I do, I'm only a man, blame the world not me,
Then the bird went tumbling off the branch and down to the ground fell she.

As I went into the city, what do you think I did see?
But a dying man upon the ground and the name of that man was me.
– Would you show me how to live, for times are bad you see,
And the world is not what it used to be, would somebody please help me?

But the only people who came along, were people who thought like me,
They blamed the world and passed me by, and that was the end of me.

Last House in the Street

A song for the children

I wrote this song after losing my way in the streets of Belfast when I was going to a concert there about twenty years ago. I'm glad to say that many things have changed since it was written – some of the words now seem dated and, for this reason, the song had slipped to the back of my mind for a while. However, in recent times I have discovered that many other people have been singing it in various corners of the earth and I've started to sing it again too, having been convinced by the people who ask to hear it, that the street and the little girl within these verses could belong to any city in the world where children suffer in the midst of conflict and violence. The song began in the Cyprus street area of Belfast although the exact place remains uncertain to me as I had lost my way completely that evening in streets that were unfamiliar. Anyway, after driving around for a while in what seemed to be ever increasing circles, I found myself on a street that seemed to be totally abandoned - broken glass and bricks strewn everywhere and on either side of this desolate scene, sightless windows and doors which had been sealed up with concrete blocks.

I was just about to turn the car yet again when, down at the far end of the street, I saw a little girl. She looked like she might have been about nine years old and, oblivious to the chaos around her, she was playing with an old tennis ball, bouncing it against the wall beside what I could now see was the last inhabited house in that street. I interrupted her game briefly to receive directions but, long after I had found my way that night, the image of the little girl stayed with me and so too did the rhythmic sound of the ball as it bounced between her hands and the wall, echoing along the empty street. A dividing wall still stands in Belfast to this day, built between Catholics and Protestants, and I continue to sing this song with the hope that, in any place of conflict, the day is coming closer when not only the walls of bricks and mortar will come down, but also the walls in people's minds.

Dear Reader

We hope you have enjoyed this book. It is one of a range of illustrated titles which we publish. Other illustrated titles aviable from Cottage Publication are:–

From our 'Paintings and stories' series

Strangford Shores
Dundalk & North Louth
Armagh
Belfast
Antrim, town & country
Inishowen
Ballynahinch and the Heart of Down

Donegal Highlands
Drogheda & the Boyne Valley
The Mournes
Fermanagh
Omagh
South Donegal

**Cottage Publications
15 Ballyhay Road
Donaghadee, Co. Down
N. Ireland, BT21 0NG**

From our 'Illustrated History & Companion' Range:–

Coleraine and the Causeway Coast
Lisburn
Ballymoney

City of Derry
Banbridge
Holywood

We can also supply prints, individually signed by the artist, of the paintings featured in the above titles as well as many other areas of Ireland.

For the more athletically inclined we can supply the following books from our illustrated walking book series

Bernard Davey's Mournes

Tony McAuley's Glens

For more details on these superb publications and to view samples of the paintings they contain, you can visit our web site at **www.cottage-publications.com** or alternatively you can contact us as follows:-

Telephone:+44 (028) 9188 8033   Fax:+44 (028) 9188 8063